MIND, HEART, HAND:

Scaffoldings of Teaching in the New Normal

by

Dr Veronica F. Guerrero
Shela Mae T. Borro
Lyneth Melissa M. Calautit
Roxanne A. Constantino
Mark Angelo R. Damo
Melody F. Damulog
Arjhonamae D. Dorotan
Jerick T. Guiang
Cindie R. Lacro
Reizel Ann L. Lucero
Ronald M. Marcos
Jonathan A. Paguirigan
Kristal Zaniah V. Ranada
Julie Ann R. Salazar
Mishell T. Sevilla
John Jufel V. Simpliciano
Chezza Maine P. Tugaoen

COPYRIGHT © 2021 MIND, HEART, HAND:
Scaffoldings of Teaching in the New Normal
By;
Dr. Veronica F. Guerrero, Shela Mae T. Borro
Lyneth Melissa M. Calautit, Roxanne A. Constantino
Mark Angelo R. Damo, Melody F. Damulog
Arjhonamae D. Dorotan, Jerick T. Guiang
Cindie R. Lacro, Reizel Ann L. Lucero
Ronald M. Marcos, Jonathan A. Paguirigan
Kristal Zaniah V. Ranada, Julie Ann R. Salazar
Mishell T. Sevilla, John Jufel V. Simpliciano
Chezza Maine P. Tugaoen

Cover Illustrator: Roberto Jose A. Domion Jr.
Cover Designer: Lance Justine D. Manuel
ISBN:
Hardbound-978-621-470-065-3
Softbound/Paperback-978-621-470-066-0
Mobile/kindle-978-621-470-067-7
For permission requests, please contact below:

Published by:
Poetry Planet Publishing House
Rosario, Pozorrubio, Pangasinan, Philippines
Contact No.: 09554960044
Email: maritesritumalta@gmail.com

MESSAGE

"Education goes on amid Covid-19 thru Deped's continuity plan"- **Philippine News Agency, December 31, 2020**
"Some students, teachers admit struggle in blended learning during pandemic"- **CNN Philippines, July 11, 2021**
"Changing the culture of learning in the Philippines"- **Manila Bulletin, August 28, 2021**
"In the middle of pandemic, digital transformation is needed toward future-ready Philippines"- **Philstar, September 3, 2021**

These are the current issues that confront teachers and learners as we approach the third decade of the 21st century. They could be a blessing or a disgrace; an opportunity or a threat; beneficial or detrimental; uplifting or degrading. **Such inevitable circumstances have set forth confusion.**

As we look at the present global scenario, people in all walks of life succumb and struggle for survival from the quagmire of pandemic. However, they have realized the significant role of their minds, hearts and hands as essential entities to contend with the demand of the new normal. Thus, this book confines documentations how these three potentials could revolutionize critical situations into favorable endeavors. **Wholesome expectations are insured at the most.**

Through our emotional attachment with these 17 masterpieces, it's not only the academe that could find comfort and relief from the phenomenon embarked on the quandary of covid19 plague; but also the entire global society. The impact of using the mind, the heart, and the hand manifests positivity and certainty in pursuing life at its best.

They serve as the scaffoldings in teaching, learning and living. **A strong confidence is developed in each individual in every undertaking.**

As reflected in the creation of this humble "obra", the master's student writers have fostered the spirit of fellowship, the essence of equality and the virtue of hope. It is an icon of their identities, convictions and aspirations. It inspires them to bring to light that there is a promising life behind the harmonious work of the mind, the heart, and the hand. **Their existence is appreciated and valued.**

"Yes. Congratulations for persevering your advocacy of teaching and reaching out the young with good thoughts, pure love and gentle tap; and building a community of mentors who serve as vanguards in promoting this ideology and in reforming many lives." – **FROM MY MIND, HEART, AND HAND.**

DR. VERONICA F. GUERRERO
Professor, Language and Literature Teaching

DEDICATION

This humble work is dedicated to our:

D-ear families for the overflowing love and inspiration;

E-nergetic friends who always cheer us up and push us to be our best;

D-etermined school administrators of the Northwestern University for the moral support;

I-nspiring teachers, dead or alive, who influenced us to be who we are now;

C-reative Filipino educators who are always working beyond expectations;

A-ccomodating book publisher for believing in our work;

T-alented students who are the reasons why we pursued for the realization of this book; and

E-minent God for being the source of all our blessings, wisdom and strength.

The Authors

PREFACE

The Covid19 pandemic has made a great paradigm shift in our Philippine educational system. Though the Department of Education is pursuing its vision to provide quality instruction among Filipino learners, we cannot deny the fact that there are still multitudes of challenges to surpass. Unless we go back to the Old Normal, we have to uphold pedagogical flexibility, creativity, and innovativeness.

This book MIND, HEART, HAND: Scaffolding of Teaching in the New Normal is an anthology of teaching experiences of seventeen (17) Ilocano educators that creatively present the effective strategies they had to overcome the teaching difficulties they encountered during the new normal. Using the MIND-HEART-HAND framework, the authors aim to inspire educators to keep their burning passion to provide quality education even in these trying times.

With these inspiring testimonies, we believe that educators will continually work beyond expectations. We envision them to believe that no virus or pandemic could ever hinder them to attain greatness and that no adversities could ever defeat a Filipino educator's creativity, versatility, and passion.

Mark Angelo R. Damo

FOREWORD

"Roses do not bloom hurriedly; for beauty, like any masterpiece, takes time to blossom."

This beautiful line from Canadian philosopher Matshona Dhliwayo would sum up the story behind this remarkable masterpiece of our versatile authors. This book MIND, HEART, HAND: Scaffoldings of Teaching in the New Normal was like a rose, watered with love, passion and commitment before it bloomed into a masterpiece.

As dean of the Vedasto J. Samonte School of Graduate Studies of the Northwestern University, I give my sincerest commendation to these 16 master's students, and their professor for coming up with such a notable achievement. Indeed, their creativity and passion in the teaching profession gave birth to this innovative accomplishment that is worthy of emulation.

Going back to the MIND, HEART and HAND, educators must really be creative to utilize them. These three (3) are very essential because if synergized, they serve as a great weapon to overcome any challenges and adversities. As a matter of fact, the effectiveness of such framework had been tested through time. Thus, it is only but proper to revisit and use it in these times of the pandemic.

Again, my warmest congratulations to these blooming writers of this generation. May your tribe increase!

Dr. Florence Ganir
Dean
Vedasto J. Samonte School of Graduate Studies
Northwestern University

TABLE OF CONTENTS

IN HARMONY
Dr. Veronica F. Guerrero

A campus heartthrob, the boy next door; yet always on his own hook with his timid smile. He prefers to sit at the center rear of the class. He is easy to spot - he is the tallest. He stoops down when our eyes meet or my forefinger goes to his direction during recitation – showing a gesture of reluctance. He is absent during scheduled reading activity. He asks for an excuse to go to the wash room when his turn to read or speak comes next.

He is such an inscrutable lad that keeps haunting me. I must discover what lies behind it. "Kindly stay after the class and help me put the English books back in the shelf." It's a sweet

imperative that no one can decline. The wide grin on his face manifests that he's alright with it.

There he goes – moving to and fro with five books at a time in his two hands, as he places them in the shelf. I notice that he even carries other books.

"Remove the books that are not English out in the shelf, please." He nods graciously. He is done. He leaves the room. He gets over with the task so well. Notwithstanding of his being unmindful probably, books in the different subjects are still in the shelves. There, my speculation is right.

The next day, I let him stay to fix the books again. He is done. He saunters towards the door. "Come here for a bit. Sit down and help me read these words."

I prepare a list of words on a sheet of coupon bond: bat, bet, bill, boy, bull, sad, sell, sit, dam, den, dim, dog. He looks at the words and turns his eyes around. He feels that no one is in the room except him and me. He stares at me apologetically.

"Ma'am, I cannot read," as he faces down. I hold his cold and shaking hands to let him feel that I understand and I'm willing to teach him how to read.

I set his schedule for thirty minutes after classes in the afternoon. I inform his adviser. We collaborate to develop his reading skill and build his confidence.

Perfect. He accepts the compromise sets before him. Everything goes so well. He is not a year level reader but at least he can read by syllable slowly and correctly. His enthusiasm to read has leveled him up into reading phrases and sentences.

Should there be more time left, I could have enriched and enhanced his reading skill. He is so happy when he sees his final grade of 75% in English.

"Thank you, ma'am," he uttered in a soft voice enveloped with life and vigor.

He waves his hand from afar as the camera clicks on and off for the class graduation picture of Batch 1995. I have not seen him since then.

This is the life in the teaching world. It calls for a great responsibility. It warrants the mind to figure out a strategy to handle a situation; the heart to embrace the fact that one needs assistance; and the hand to hold a shivering handclasp. If all of these work together as one and in harmony, it can save a soul.

VERSATILITY: A TEACHER'S GREATEST STRENGTH

Shela Mae T. Borro

A lot of people materialize education as a 'passion'. I, myself, never thought I would be one. I do not believe in chances but, I believe in 'no choice'. Many are the reasons why others become a teacher or an educator. Some believe that it's an escape from criticisms due to high respect for teachers. Some believe that they are a step higher than the mediocre because they've experienced judgment and belittling. Some believe that it's an escape from poverty. But, I say, it's one direction. I had no choice but to crawl into this path made for me because my mother said that this is a practical course and it is very easy to look for a job when you are a teacher. But things get different when the 'passion' they are all talking about, already burns in my heart.

This profession is both a career and a responsibility. My first year of teaching started in July 2020 with Covid-19 rampant. And I tell you, it is a roller-coaster ride. As I go over this profession, all the domains of my being were tested especially when the pandemic occurred. I've asked myself and sought some help from my friends on how I would fully apply all these in harmony. Thanks to the collaborations I had with my co-teachers and the empowerment I received from my friends in order for me to survive my first year of teaching.

The Mind. John Milton said, "The mind is its own place, and in itself, can make a heaven of Hell, a hell of Heaven." The mind is powerful so I chose to fix myself, manage my time, and strategize in making my learning activities more effective. We are called educators to be the fountain of knowledge and by this, it is always important to make use of engaging activities even if the mode of learning is more on the use of self-learning modules. Pandemic is already a stressful word and we should devise ways to not be an additional cause of learners' struggle in learning. There are lots of cognitive stimulation activities that are available on the internet, we just have to choose the ones that fit our subject matter. Let's prove that one of our strengths is versatility.

The Heart. We are entitled as 'second parents' of our learners. The responsibilities rely on our hands to find the needs, interests, talents, and skills of our learners. Well, finding is not enough, we should go the extra mile to hone these talents and skills for they can use these in building their dreams. We should inculcate in them the values that help them develop their skills and personality. I always remind my students that life is what you make it. This line is always been the line of my favorite high school teacher and she inspires me until now. I've always been looking up to her. I told myself that she is exactly the teacher whom I want to be in the future and now, I want to become the teacher that my students wish to be in the future.

The Hand. When it comes to the teaching-learning process, the hand symbolizes the execution of learning plans. The journey of teaching during this pandemic plays a big role in becoming an innovative and creative educator. I always keep in mind that the learning of my students should not end with the piece of paper that they have, the same goes with the four corners of the classroom. So, as an MKO (More Knowledgeable Other), it is my duty to offer a helping hand to these learners to somehow make them feel that we are their partners in achieving their dreams. We let them know that we are clapping and celebrating their achievements and successes.

Indeed, teaching is a well-rounded profession. It covers all aspects of the totality of your being. It might be difficult but difficult-fulfilling. I always challenge myself to make teaching a wonderful fairytale that my learners would enjoy. In that way, they will all participate and will all learn. I will always be grateful for this profession. It led me to prosperously motivate and inspire others to have a mind, a heart, and a hand willing to help at all cause that I never thought would come and would happen.

PANDEMIC DEJA VU

Lyneth Melissa M. Calautit

The world today is so much different from the past. It has now become exhausting, depressing, unhealthy, and most of all threatening. It was so sudden that all of the things we usually do are now out of our reach. As I travel back by memory, I can see the happy faces of my students sharing stories under the mango trees, along the corridors and untidy classrooms. Days of being in school were not perfect. There were fatiguing days as well as the arduous school works to accomplish. Undeniably, being with our learners in person is a delight to us. Sad to say, our present no longer empowers us.

This pandemic has taught us many things. I, for one, have a lot of things learned and have been learning as the days pass by.

I remember the day when the unforeseen emergence of the Covid-19 muddled the world. I thought I am never able to get hold of my teaching career. That the world is ending and all dreams have concluded. However, we are all created by the love of God. He molded us with an unparalleled understanding that we could be able to comprehend the circumstances. Our superiors have made things possible to help every educator pursue the task we are called for, cultivating young minds.

With the swift change of setting and condition, we all should be able to endure these changes too. Teachers are flexible and tenacious, and we are always ready to take whatever life bestows us. The rapid change indeed has also challenged our mechanism in action. We are first-hand on this. Therefore, there should be harmony of the mind, heart, and hands.

The mind as the wellspring of knowledge should foster well-planned, relevant, and suitable teaching and learning strategies. The fact is that our learners deserve to be well-guided, so we always make sure we have imparted learnings and realizations at the end of the day. The mind is the control of what we wanted to carry out.

On the other hand, the heart feels the interest and needs of our learners. It is the channel of empathy and compassion. I have encountered different types of students. There are these with abilities that are incomparable but worse off in life. There are lavish but never have the keenness to be instructed.

Whoever they are and whatever life status they belong to, they all deserve our solicitude and warmth. Today we serve as their fortress against depression to whatever caused it. We are their tower of strength while they realize the significance of education to their lives and our society. Let our heart feel their need and let us make them feel they are needed. In the first place, we care for them, the salient portion of our society.

The hands are the one who performs all the conceivable notion about the teaching-learning process. The application of our thoughts is through our hands. For what is a mind full of magnificent views if not executed. At present, we are flexed by too many functions to carry out both at home and school. Despite it, our love for our vocation subjugates. This affliction has proven that the hands are the dominant medium of help. Our hands not only comfort a weary heart, carry out our actions and practices during the new normal phase of education.

The mind, the heart, and the hand should be in harmony as we fulfill our duties. I believe that these three cannot function without the other. Although there are people who do not believe in our efforts and intentions, we should keep the faith in ourselves and keep the thought that we are this country's help in shaping the future.

TRIANGULATING EDUCATION

Roxanne A. Constantino

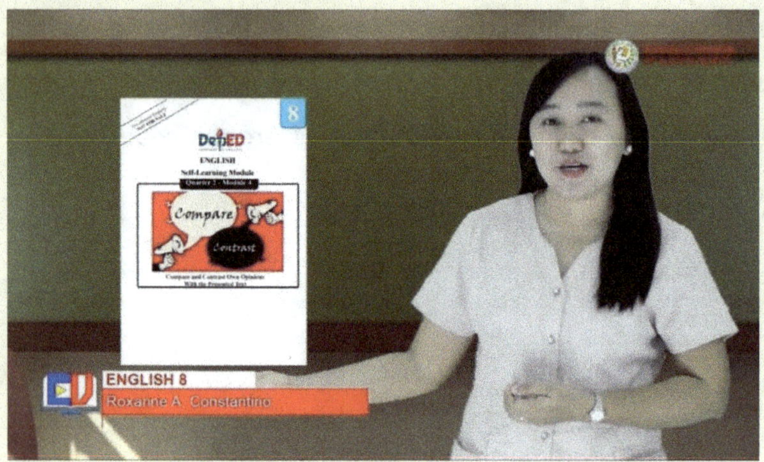

It has been more than a year since we were shaken by a terrible news about the never-before-seen global disease called CoViD19, which caused unimaginable destructions and disruptions in the lives and livelihood of people. Numerous changes were made that we had to adapt to the so-called New Normal.

As far as education is concerned, it is also deemed necessary to transform face to face learning modality to distance learning modality to safeguard the students and the teachers. Hence, teachers and students alike voyage in an unchartered sea.

Transitioning from face to face classes to virtual classes is no easy feat. As a teacher, I have been exhausting as many resources as I could possibly find to educate myself how to survive this new normal in education.

Our battle with the pandemic is far from over, therefore, we must embrace the changes made in our education curriculum by teaching using the MIND, HEART and HAND. Let us dive in and get immersed...

USING THE MIND. Nothing can be less inspiring than the monotony of always doing the same thing. Truly, as a teacher, I strive to improve my teaching strategies and techniques by collaborating with my colleagues and attending webinars to welcome new ideas that will further help me deliver instruction to my students. I also exert time and effort in crafting contextualized lessons and designing interesting competency-aligned activities and differentiated tasks because I aim to see the light bulb moments in my students' minds.   USING THE HEART. Teaching, as they say, is a work of heart and the best teachers teach not only from the book but also from the heart. While it is true that a teacher's job is to share knowledge with the students, it is also true that one should not disregard to inspire and touch their lives. Similarly, it is always important to build relationships with them especially in these trying times. Whenever I possibly can, I do home visitations to my students, particularly those who do not have the means to participate in our online classes, those who are not tech-savvy and those who have apprehensions in the current learning modality, to provide them assistance and motivation. Teaching may be challenging and difficult yet I still love going the extra mile for them and looking out for their interests and needs. After all, I feel rewarded when I see them thrive.

USING THE HAND. It is impossible for a teacher not to get things done. Just like any other teacher, I also work long hours to produce meaningful and creative instructional materials for my students to easily grasp what is being taught to them. Although making supplementary learning materials somehow feels exhausting, I still continue doing it for my students.

Our students deserve the best of us. They deserve the same inspired, passionate, joyful and energetic teacher that they had during the face to face classes and during these virtual classes. Thus, we, teachers, must teach our students using the mind, heart and hand then we will find ourselves receiving much more than we are giving.

THE ANATOMY OF AN UNSUNG HERO

Mark Angelo R. Damo

"Gelo, teachers are unsung heroes. Some do not really appreciate their worth. But do not be discouraged. Synergize your mind, heart and hands and be a great teacher."

These words from a great mentor, the late Dr. Vicente A. Bonoan, still reverberates in my mind. How can I ever forget these golden nuggets of wisdom from him? The way he spoke and looked at me in the eyes unveiled his being a passionate and dedicated teacher. He was so inspiring that all of us in the academe (where we worked before) gave him our respect.

The Covid-19 pandemic has brought a lot of changes and challenges most especially in the field of education. The government's desire to pursue education despite of the pandemic, gave birth to what we call the New Normal in Education. However, based on my experiences as a public school teacher, it is not only the internet connectivity and the educational gadgets that are needed. I came to realize that Dr. Vic's "synergy of the mind, heart, and hand" must be practiced in order to hurdle the various challenges of our Philippine educational sector. The solutions should start from us teachers and cascade it to our students so that they will also share these to their immediate communities. Yes, solving the issue should be in a domino effect.

So what really makes up a great teacher? Let us dissect the very structure of a great teacher by expounding what "synergy of the mind, heart and hand" means.

The mind, the heart and the hands are interconnected with each other. These three essentials make up the anatomy of an effective teacher. Let us see the individual functions of each part:

First is the mind. The mind creates the concept, conceives and selects the content, and sets the standards. It chooses the teaching strategies to be used. As the control center, it generates a plan or a blueprint of what must be done inside the classroom.

Second is the heart. This vital part is the one that regulates the mind. It humanizes the concept, content and standards set by the mind. The heart is responsible in what we call- "value integration in our classes". Remember that we do not just teach knowledge, but also "essential values" that would make our learners globally competitive. The emotional aspect of our learners is vital in their holistic development.

Third is the hand. The hand creates and implements. It is responsible in the crafting of the teaching materials and resources. Also, the power of touch or haptics have a positive psychological effect to our students. The hand can show comfort and motivation to our students.

All parts are equally important for they play significant roles to really create a prototype of an effective teacher. Thus, these three should synergize with each other so that a positive impact be achieved. The mind is useless if it does not connect to the heart and the hand, and vice versa. The mind, heart and hand must work as a whole rather than individual parts.

As a public shool teacher, I came to realize that when we activate this "synergy of the mind, heart and hand in us", we can be more productive. I believe that all of us have beautiful concepts and ideas. However, they are just kept in the mind because some of us lack the confidence to turn them into reality. There was no cascading of these concepts and ideas into the heart and the hands. Thus, no positive impact has been made.

So, when I realized this, I, together with my colleagues Mr. John Jufel Simpliciano and Dr. Sherwin Palaspas, proposed to our school principal a way on how we could ease the academic burdens of our students in the New Normal. This innovation was dubbed as Project BANGA (Bringing Assessment in the New Normal to Greatness through Academic Ease) which aimed to produce uniform activity sheets given to students for them to answer. The strengths of this project is that it addresses the individual differences and learning styles of students, it uses contextualization as an approach, and it serves as a great opportunity for teachers to be authors of these printed activity sheets.

In its pilot implementation, the Project BANGA has earned positive feedback from students, parents, teachers and other stakeholders. The great support of our school administration headed by our school principal Mrs. Eliza C. Vedania helped us to make the concept a reality.

As closing, we need to remember that all of us teachers can make a positive difference in the world. When we entered the teaching profession, we were fueled by our passion, dedication and commitment to transform our learners into the best they can be. So, we should not settle for less because there are endless possibilities. At the end of the day, we will all go back to what Dr. Vic said that we are the unsung heroes of yesterday, today, and tomorrow.

SEEING THE BRIGHT SIDE OF TEACHING IN THE PANDEMIC

Melody F. Damulog

"My mind, my heart and my hands will continue to nurture young students to develop their reading abilities and to help them become their best versions." -message

"Reading is boring. Reading is hard." These are the mindsets of many students that every language teacher wants to change. We want to teach our students to approach learning the language in an enthusiastic, authentic and flexible way. However, the temporary closure of schools brought by Covid-19 Pandemic hampered teachers to execute teaching reading in the typical way. We were challenged to think of ways on how to reach these learners who struggle in reading. We had sleepless nights thinking of what modality we should use to assist our learners, knowing that there are many of them who need help. We became helpless for a moment. We were doubtful on whether to continue the reading program or not because of possible exposure to a deadly disease.

Nonetheless, as a dedicated teacher, my heart really pushed me to the bottom to teach reading in the pandemic. I am so lucky that my head had been very supportive in the planning and implementation of this endeavor. I was able to develop a school-based program "LAKBAY BASA SA MUNDO NG TEKNOLOHIYA" an open blended reading program for frustrated, instructional learners and interested readers. With full support from my principal and careful planning of what and how to do – from preparation of materials and testing of the modality, my hard work has indeed been paying off. At first, there were ups and downs. Some even questioned me if it's hard and challenging. But, with positive mindset and visualization of my target goal, everything became so successful. It's amazing how parents took part in the reading process. In fact, they enjoyed each playful reading and writing activities I had prepared for them. I also utilized messenger for my online and offline classes and every activity was a meaningful preservation of learning.   The struggling readers are now independent readers of the language. Feedbacks from parents are worth-taking because of the many thanks they had sent to me. The most amazing part is that my learners were given chances to be guided by their parents while on the reading process, moments which in typical days were seldom observed.

Yet, I do not seat on my laurels, so to speak. I continue to join different seminars and trainings and post graduate studies to improve my teaching techniques. Meeting the challenges in teaching reading through painstaking study and preparation will help me a lot to continue what I have started. I will pour myself into researching much better ways to improve my reading program and I will continue to help my school to have an even better reputation in nurturing the reading abilities of my students. Most importantly, I put God as the center of my profession because I know that with him, my success in teaching is one hundred percent guaranteed.

Truly, if a teacher has the mind that plans carefully, the heart that loves and truly cares for her learners; when they work together, the art of hands becomes so beautiful and successful.

THE FOUNDATION FOR BETTER EDUCATION IN THE NEW NORMAL

Arjhonamae D. Dorotan

Covid-19 Pandemic brought us a lot of challenges that we thought would never happen. In this time of new normal, there are rules that have been implemented, safety protocols and procedures that we need to follow and most of all, limited movements and gatherings that surely have an impact on our social life. These are some adjustments that have been circulating in our society up to this moment, where we do not know when this will stop. We do not know what this will bring us or where this brings us. Many lives now were crashed, doctors and nurses that were tired but kept on fighting. These are some serious dilemmas that have been attacking us, but we do not know how to solve and stop them.

Learning in the new normal is a challenge for the teachers, students and even parents. The new way of learning brought by the pandemic can be an additional challenge during this tough time and led us to a more complicated set up in education. Took us a lot of patience and dedication for us to deliver the lesson. But nevertheless, in every undertaking, there must be something that we must learn and reflect on, that even in this time of uncertainty we must do our job as an educator. We must not forget the reason why we choose to be in this type of profession and that is to share knowledge and ideas, not only to the young generations but also to all individuals who are willing to learn. But how can we share these ideas and knowledge during pandemic? This now will enter the Three Foundation for Better Education in the New Normal: the HEAD, HEART AND HAND.

There are a lot of ways that we can use as a technique in teaching, but I do believe that using the HEAD, HEART AND HAND, we can deliver the lesson in a more effective way, using the Head as cognitive, the Heart as an affective and the Hand as psychomotor. These three domains in learning can be an effective formula in teaching especially in this time of new normal. These three should be connected to each other because what the Head thinks will be the Heart desires to do and will be implemented by the Hands. When the Head where our brain thinks of ideas and knowledge, we intend to deliver and share to our learners passionately and effectively. Where we use our hands to give gestures to provide more impact and effectiveness in delivering the lesson. Moreover, as an educator, we intend that our learners will not just bring the ideas and knowledge to their minds or head but also, we want them to feel and affect their lives what they have learned and surely be implemented by them at the end of the lesson.

The Head, Heart and Hand helps us also to deliver the lesson to our learners for them to gain knowledge, skills and mindset that are necessary in this new normal set-up. It helps us to ensure the quality of learning that we will provide to our learner's despite this pandemic. At first, it's difficult, but we need to cope up with the changes we have in order to survive. This change also is an opportunity for us to learn more. To be creative and innovative in implementing learning ideas that will not just be absorbed by the head but stay in their heart and surely used by the hands.

EXCELLENT TEACHER

Jerick T. Guiang

Change is inevitable. Many experts in the academe saw the need to execute novel strategies to mitigate the predicament changes and issues that are detrimental to the roles of the teacher, the learner, and the community. These strategies promote learning cultures that improve the students' holistic development beneficial to their lifelong learning. According to the Journal of Senka Gazibara (2013), lifelong learning integrates the three learning domains: cognitive (head), affective (heart), and practical (hands). The concoction of these three domains is imperative to enumerate and solve the problems evident in contemporary education. The three domains are significant for educators to become competent in cultivating globally competitive individuals.

From a teacher's perspective, with all the changes and uncertainties happening to the world and the education system, being in the manacles of fear is not a great help. Instead, we should have the heart, the head, and the hand that shows passion, effective strategy, and action in teaching.

As I write this narrative, I have been in the teaching profession for five years, have been through changes and experiences, and still cannot be called an excellent educator. It is because I know for myself that I am not exceptional in all three areas. Despite the hardships and frustrations, I still choose to be resilient because the passion drives me to be a teacher. Reaching out and extending warmth to my students illuminate care and assurance that they are being taken care of. Knowing how they feel and how's their relationship with their peers might be beyond what I signed for but education is not only limited to the four walls of the classroom after all. Being passionate is not enough. Effective teaching is the ability to produce strategic ways that amend all the challenges and setbacks in the learning process. I look at these challenges as opportunities to be more expert in the pedagogy and content of the lesson that I am delivering to my students. I familiarize myself with the concepts that hold my students back and dig into more solutions, information, and knowledge to connect them to the bigger world. Education is not only limited to the four walls of the classroom after all. My actions do not always result positively and the way I want them to be. A mistake will always be there and avoiding it to happen is not wrong at all. As stress becomes part of me being a teacher, I manage and organize my time surely and accurately to create a positive environment for my students and my colleagues. I avoid tasks to pile up so that I can still lend a hand to people who need help. Teaching is not only a job to do and education is not only limited to the four walls of the classroom after all.

I am not an excellent teacher and I guess will never be because as teacher, I am also a student who is continuously learning, committing mistakes, and striving to be better every day. Thus, for as teachers, may our heart illuminates love, may our head be the beacon of hope, and may our hands be extended from the terrains to the mountains and the waves reaching for excellence.

EPIPHANY OF TEACHING

Cindie R. Lacro

The teacher plays a vital role in society. They mold children to become productive citizens of the country. But how do we measure the quality of a teacher? Is it the years she spent teaching, the lengthiness of patience she has, the effectiveness of her lessons, or the affections she's giving to her students? Well, these are few things you possess as a teacher. But have you ever asked yourself, what makes a teacher a TEACHER?

There are three body parts needed in teaching effectively. These are the head, the hand, and the heart.

Plan as the Head in Teaching. As an educator, you know that before class starts, you should prepare a lesson plan. Aside from making a lesson plan, you should also have a plan for the betterment of yourself and your students! There should be strategies and techniques you will be using to achieve your goals for your students at the end of the school year. Be physically and mentally prepared. Physically, you must have proper grooming. You can set the mood according to the lesson you are going to discuss. Students will be more active in class if they connect the topic to real life. Mentally, you should know what you are teaching. Make sure that you will give all the knowledge that a student must learn, correctly. Be sure of what you are going to teach because one mistake can change the learners' perception.

Action as the Hand in Teaching. Before the world went locked down, there are lots of teaching styles in delivering the lesson that can catch students' interests. You can use a traditional one and a modern one. But during the pandemic, some of those strategies are not applicable. But, new teaching strategies came out. You can also make your version of teaching. If it's effective then, you may share it with your colleagues. Try different teaching styles so that you can assess what style is best for that topic.

Fondness as the Heart in Teaching. Educators who are fond of teaching and have good relationships with their students use their hearts in teaching. They are more attached to their students. If you are very fond of teaching, you are also very fond of learning. Students nowadays are technology born. So do not be afraid of doing new things. Even if a problem arises, you must try to face it. Just like the pandemic, wherein face-to-face teaching is not allowed, you should make new strategies and adjust yourself for them.

We all have our ways to measure our effectiveness to the students. But if the head, heart, and hand work together, we are all complete packaged teachers. We are effective teachers if we are confident that we can make a good impact on them. The question is: "Teacher, what makes you a TEACHER?"

THE EPITOME OF EFFECTIVE TEACHING

Reizel Ann L. Lucero

Education plays a significant role in every person's life. Even in times of crisis this should not hinder to pursue and achieve one's dreams in life. This pandemic brought a lot of changes in our curriculum which really affects education turning into new normal from face-to-face to online/modular learning, but we need to continue teach and touch the lives of the young minds. We, teachers are indeed an epitome of knowledge who's responsible for nurturing many lives, a source of inspiration who makes learning a continuous process by Caring, Understanding, Communicating and believing that we are not only the facilitator of learning but a second parent too.

A Caring Teacher nurtures the talents and encourages one to aspire to achieve more. Being a great teacher, we should care about our students. Distance between us and our learners during this time of crisis should not be stopped but rather we should encourage them to succeed and are committed to helping them achieve their goals. Investing ourselves in our students creates a positive atmosphere in our classroom that can enhance our relationship with our students and makes them feel important. Also, students feel better about themselves if they feel that we as their teacher has taken a genuine interest in them; they are motivated, and stronger self-assurance can make it easier for the student to challenge themselves academically and even emotionally. With younger students, away from their parents they really need special attention for guidance, so as a teacher it is also one of our duties to care about the welfare of our students (holistically) if necessary. That's why our classroom also must be seen as a caring and supportive place with a sense of belonging, most importantly that we are in the middle of pandemic we should show our care to our students. Every student must feel respected, valued and heard regardless of who and what they are. Giving them the support for learning by welcoming their questions and encouraging exploration is very important for us to do.

A Teacher understands the students better than they themselves do. Getting to know who our students are as individuals can help us to provide an inclusive, respectful and accepting classroom environment. This will not only help to keep our students highly engaged in learning but will also provide a safe space for them during tough times that will encourage them to open and seek support when needed. Some of our students may feel too shy to speak up in classroom discussions and may not enjoy large-group tasks or volunteering to deliver presentations as much as another student might. Instead, these students could feel more comfortable expressing their views through online forums, one-on-one conversations or via messenger chat. Understanding our students' interests will help us to provide the quality learning opportunities. We have diverse learners who came from all walks of life so we should be considerate enough about their strengths and weaknesses.

Good communication is what it takes to be an effective teacher. Delivering the lesson well and speaking fluently in front our learners doesn't mean that we are effective communicators it also needs to help build and foster a safe learning environment where students can thrive, prosper and learn freely. Communication between teachers and students is not always about talking but also sympathizing. A good example is when we were still having the face-to-face, we must create a safe and supportive environment where our students feel comfortable to open and express their thoughts and ideas. Moving around the classroom and getting involved with the students will create less of a student-teacher feel. By moving away from the front of the classroom and joining them either at their desks to discuss ideas and getting involved in small discussions will help them feel more comfortable. Oftentimes, we forget to mention when a student has performed well in the classroom instead focus on the negative aspects such as bad behavior, poor attendance and others. These can have significant effects and demoralize students. Although negative feedback can create positive outcomes by helping students to improve, giving positive feedback is a necessary part of promoting effective communication in the classroom. Allowing them to share their feedback on lessons or teaching styles shows that you appreciate and value their opinion as well as helping to improve learning. And now that we are in a new normal education, we can be a good communicator by allowing themselves to feel that they opinions and ideas are always appreciated and welcomed despite the distance we have.

MARKS WITH GENUINE CAUSES

Ronald M. Marcos

The artistic hands carve lessons to value the meaning of life.

The brilliant head instills lessons that inspire a knowledge-driven mind.

The compassionate heart engraves values that will create virtuous and God-fearing individuals.

Covid-19 has changed the landscape of the educational system. In these trying times, where face-to-face learning is discouraged, it has become a challenge for teachers to impart knowledge to students through new modes of instruction such as virtual, blended, or remote type. Teachers also struggle with how they accurately and effectively assess their students' academic performance. On the other hand, learners are mentally exhausted grasping the needed information and learning inputs from their teachers. Teachers as frontliners in the teaching process should be armed with artistic hands, brilliant minds, and compassionate hearts to facilitate meaningful learning among students amidst pandemic.

The mark of a comforting and caring hand. As a teacher, I use my hands if I want to do something especially the things I love. This pandemic opened opportunities for me to craft and develop modules, activity sheets, and scripts for radio-based instruction and educational television. I became an instant writer and broadcaster. My hands never get tired writing and writing just to create interesting lessons for students using various modalities. I use these hands as essential instruments to better my teaching activities. Moreover, it is these same hands that I use to demonstrate compassion to our stricken students. My hands are widely-opened, extending support and assistance, tapping my students' weakening shoulders for them to be strong in fighting against all odds. It's a gesture of oneness and motivation to face the challenges of the new normal. I see these artistic hands as weapons to teach lessons about real life and comfort the afflicted in these difficult times.

The mark of a compassionate heart.   In my years of service in the field, the true passion of teaching has been engraved in my heart - LOVE. It is with love that adds vivid and vibrant colors in teaching. This crisis made me realize the importance of sharing and treating everyone as family. More than ever, this new normal has taught to treat others, regardless of their backgrounds, with selfless love.   In fact, I spearheaded the S.H.A.R.E to C.A.R.E. Program (Service with a Heart And Render it to Everyone to Create an Active, Resilient, and Empowered Community) and I felt so fortunate that God made me an instrument to help others. This is the prize of conducting home visitation to my students to know them better and provide necessary assistance to the needy and less fortunate. In teaching and coaching, I make sure to offer a compassionate heart. And I always advocate these principles: 1) Let love circle the air in the teaching-learning process, and 2) let our students feel our love that will forever a mark in their hearts.

The mark of a comprehending mind. I don't teach only by the book, but I share real life stories and lessons with my students which definitely hit their inner core and paved way to a richer and better insights about life and the world. I make learning as fun, exciting, and engaging as possible, deviating from the so-called "old-school" way of mentoring. I believe in diverse ways of teaching: printed modular to online modalities, visual to kinesthetic activities, basic to complex inputs and assessments. I consider differentiated instructions. I encourage students to flaunt their true self, their true personality, and most importantly, I design classroom activities that unleash the greatest potentials of my students because I believe that when a student lives with no fears or judgments, this world can be better than what we perceive it to be for them. With this, we create critical and creative citizens of the world, ready to participate in intellectual discussions and poised to create remarkable solutions to global issues and problems.

This plight we are facing has accelerated multifarious kinds of worries and anxieties. But I, as a teacher, chose to be a warrior and not a worrier. Knowing that I am exposing myself with the dreaded virus, I defied the odds and made sure that my oath in the noblest profession be fulfilled.

Indeed, this pandemic has taught us many things: creativity, flexibility, discipline, care and compassion for others, and a stronger relationship with God. Teaching in this time of pandemic has forced me to go beyond the four walls of the classroom. It has encouraged me to walk through the walls of the community to have a better understanding of the real situation of our learners. It has empowered me to upgrade my teaching instruments to meet with the demands of the time and the pressing needs of our students. Even more, it has inspired me to rise above the threats of the corona virus to serve our students and the bigger community with a caring and comforting hand, a compassionate heart, and a comprehending mind. And in the end, I will achieve the crown of being the best teacher a student could ever have. Truly, I will always be their Sir Marcos: A teacher that leaves a MARk with genuine CaUSes.

THE MAKING OF FUTURE LEADERS

Jonathan A. Paguirigan

Being a teacher has always been a great challenge. The responsibilities that rest on my shoulders are overwhelming; some are laid beforehand and some arrive by surprise. With these, there is no other path for me to take than to work hard and achieve progress every single day especially that I teach in the tertiary level where students are older, more mature and idealistic than secondary learners. It is therefore a need to have a harmonious application of the different domains of learning. Thus, the birth of new leaders comes to the fore.

First is the MIND. I need to be equipped with appropriate and enough knowledge with regards to the subject matter that I am teaching. Having a mastery of the subject matter will help me do my job better and easier. I need to patiently do as many readings and research as possible in order to come up with a richer and wider perspective about the lesson. But, having all these is not enough. I also need to be creative, especially in the conduct of my class each day. Varying styles and techniques has to be applied in every class depending on the program of the learners, considering that they came from diverse background and varied levels of thinking. The same is applied to assessment and evaluation so as to achieve equality and equity among my students to make sure that their cognitive domain are properly and well-fed is accordance to their needs.

Second is the HEART. Whatever I intend for my learners in the cognitive domain has to be coupled with a heart. Dubbed as a second parent to learners, the responsibility and the expectation is too high that is why I need to take the role heartily. Aside from being a role model and mentor to them, they have to feel that I am their dad in the classroom. Although they are more mature and older, they still need my affection as their teacher because it helps them to strive better in their class performance. The psychological and emotional aspect of their learning has to be provided with utmost importance and has to be unyielding and serious. Putting my heart in the way I treat them is a huge boost and motivation to them to strive harder and get inspired to succeed. In like manner, telling them to put their heart in whatever they do will provide them the opportunity to feel the relevance of their learning. Another technique that I usually do in my class is to hit their weakness- their PARENTS. Reminding them of the sacrifices and hardships that their parents are going through is the best way for them to focus and reflect. There are even times that their tears fell in front of my face because they sincerely feel the words that I am trying to convey to them. In addition, always reminding them to study well, to do their assigned task, to take care all the time, to avoid vices, to call or text me if they need to ask something or even if they have a problem and to encourage them to pray everyday is not too much on my part as a teacher. And at this point, the word 'work' is momentarily defied, but is replaced by a more meaningful word called 'father'.

Finally is the HAND. In order to complete the ingredients that our learners need to be equipped with, putting all the knowledge and the heart into their hands has to be realized. As stated by Immanuel Kant that the hand is the visible part of the brain, the physical practice and application of what was learned has to be applied by the hand. In the work field, the hand will be mostly utilized. Thus, the psychomotor skills has to be learned, trained and mastered. Moreover, the hand is not only used to do things what the lesson dictates, but it is also an instrument to extend the heart for others- to their family, classmates, friends, teachers, and community, which will surely be carried by them for the rest of their lives. The humility and love that the heart and mind dictates takes a simple touch of the hand to achieve it. At the end of the day, our students may come to realize that having all the successes and the wealth in this world will not justify contentment and happiness, but the humility and love that their hand have extended for others. As for me, I use my hand not just to show them to do things, but also, to show that they are well-taken care of.

With these simple ways of treatment I had to my students and the foundation that I tried to lay for them, I am confident that they will succeed and become exemplary future leaders. I sincerely thank God for leading me to this profession. It is truly fulfilling and it brings exceptional joy to my heart.

A WORDSMITH'S TRIUNE

Kristal Zaniah V. Ranada

Year 2020 was my first year of teaching and I had no idea what 'real-world' teaching is all about. Being a teacher in today's situation is quite challenging. I cannot deny the fact that I was not prepared for what is yet to come for me as I gamble with this profession. Every time I wake up, I make sure I am set to indulge in new things and will try my best to learn and flourish from these things.

This new way of learning led me to become more patient, creative, resourceful and competent at the same time. With my first year of teaching I have learned that teaching is not just talking and giving information to your students in the four corners of your classroom, instead being a teacher must be flexible all the time.

One of the things that I began establishing as I entered teaching is my head. I know that I would be meeting pain-in-the-head learners but with proper guidance I know that they will learn and reflect from their actions. Everything can be solved in a manner properly communicated. Building their trust will they only truly find respect not just to you as a teacher but to others and to themselves.

Also, I considered preparing my character and emotions. Before, I had no temper when it comes to learners' misbehaviors. But then I realized, I was like them before and now I understand why my teachers acted that way during our time. Adding flame to the fire won't stop the fire. Learn their backgrounds and understand where these behaviors are coming from. Make family background checking because it might be one of the causes if not the main cause. I have learned to gather these experiences and apply them in teaching to make a healthy environment valued by these clienteles.

Not all learners are intelligent and capable in every aspect. Wide understanding is very much needed as I've seen many of them suffer. A teacher is not just there to teach and to discipline but to offer a helping hand to the needy. I've learned the importance of giving because that is the least thing that we could do for them to feel comfortable in our shade.

Life of a teacher is simple but it becomes meaningful the moment we realize how much of a responsibility we carry the moment we step out of our homes. What's important is that we were able to help these young hopefuls in achieving their dreams despite the many challenges we face and criticisms we hear. Like what the Fox said to the Little Prince, "It is only with the heart that one can see rightly: what is essential is invisible to the eye." The public may not see our efforts but the child does and that's what matters the most.

WHEN THE HEAD THINKS, THE HEART AFFECTS, THE HAND FEELS

Salazar, Julie Ann

Education has many different implications. Others feel that it is the path to prosperity; others believe that it is a question of recognition; still others believe that education is what makes a person worthy of being copied by more; and yet others believe that education is the path to achieving one's life goals.

Educators serve as instrument in providing quality and effective education to the young and innocent mind of the learners. They reach out even in the far-flung areas just to give what the learners' need, day in and day out. They don't stop thinking of new strategies on how to deliver the best quality of education to their learners.

When the Head thinks...

An educator is equipped with proper knowledge on what she is going to deliver and how she is going to send such to her learners. She never fails to contemplate on the knowledges that she is going to share to her learners. She also carefully thinks on the things that she is going to give to her learners. She knows the right and correct the wrong in order to educate properly her learners.

the Heart affects...

She teaches not just to share knowledge but also to affect the lives of her learners. She became aware of the needs of her learners. She thinks of the proper way on how to deliver the information whole heartedly without hesitation. She compensates to the feeling of her learners and show them the right way to become a successful individual.

the Hand feels...

She already knows the information, she also knows the right way to deliver, she now then uses gestures in order for her learners to understand what she wants to tell them. These non-verbal communications make her more confident in delivering the message she wants her learners to have. She points the board if she wants to emphasize, she claps her hand when she hears a good answer and embrace them to let her learners that she is happy with them.

When the head thinks, it evolves on the other systems of the body, they follow. However, in education, it contemplates the heart and the hand. This is to accentuate the teaching-learning process. For when the head thinks, the heart affects, then the hand feels.

THREE ACTS FOR A TRANSFORMATIVE EDUCATION

Mishell Sevilla

We all want to be effective. It makes a great difference when we feel that we are developing minds, touching hearts, and working hand in hand in the production of well-transformed individuals. Teaching is best rewarding when we think, feel and work.

Teachers are called to have a direct impact on their students. Teachers can see their work in action and see the changes they affect. They want to help people. And as teachers aspire to educate and to affect positive change, there has to be the effective collaboration of the mind, heart, and hand for a transformative education.

I think this pandemic has brought many challenges that gave me also an opportunity to discover more of myself and to have a deeper view on what this new normal set-up of education demands. This made me think newer teaching and learning techniques based on digital learning tools and technologies that allows me to see connections towards my students. While engaging in such learning opportunities keep on thinking about my students, their needs, and interests, I need also to think about myself, the issues I am facing and how I can apply that learning into my context so that my students and I learn from each other.

I feel that teaching is a passion that allows me to be resilient even when things are not going my way. Oh, how I love to teach, but the different preparation, challenging conduct of classes and internet issues in this new normal gets me frustrated sometimes. I love my students, but there are a few who test my patience. In online classes, there are those who turn off their camera, mute themselves and then go on their phone to play online games or message with friends and others. In printed modular distance learning, there are those who do not take modules wholeheartedly. They copy answers from others without reading the lesson and even say they are not learning from the modules but still need to show up with a smile that is coming from a cheerful heart. The more challenges, the more I am motivated to do means to get in touch with them.

I work in a smart preparation to start motivating my students to work for their dreams no matter what it is. During this new normal where everything seems tough, I should work with my students and other stakeholders to be able for them to identify the essential things they need to do for a brighter future which is already the application of the information they have learned. I should not get tired getting myself updated with the new trends in education that may help improve my role as a teacher to transform the world by making learning exciting and by making quality education accessible amidst health crisis we are facing right now.

Truly, this new normal reminds us again to think, feel and work to see the positive change on the face of education through transformative education with the effective use of mind, heart, and hand.

R(EA)ICH

John Jufel Valdez Simpliciano

Mind...Heart...Hands...In the world of education, these three important things serve as great weapons for us, the teachers, to fight for the future of our students. We always incorporate what we think, feel and do into all the lessons that we deliver to them. Through the synergy of these 3 great weapons, we are helping our students achieve academic success while being happy, healthy and contended with their achievements.

Through this realization, I never hesitated to accept the responsibility given by our School Principal, Mrs. Eliza C. Vedania, to become a Reading Coordinator of the school. Together with my fellow language teachers, we are challenged to enhance the Remedial Reading Program so that we can reach out to poor readers and nonreader and give them wider opportunities to improve their reading skills. With the continuous support of our School Principal, Parents Teachers Association and other stakeholders, our Remedial Reading Program won First Runner Up in the 2019 Region I - Best Implementer of Bawat Bata Bumabasa last March 2019.

After receiving this success, an unfortunate event happened. The whole world was in chaos because the Covid -19 broke out. Everything was in total disarray, and the economic, social, political, and educational system worldwide were out of hand.

Despite of this unforeseen dilemma, we still strived to find ways to reach out to these students. We continue to discover their obstacles so that way we may be able to tailor our ways to support them. We never stopped to show compassion so that they will always feel that there is no more important than to share love with one another. We always make them realize that they are the captain of their own ships.

No virus can stop us in assisting our poor readers to improve not only their reading skills but also their selves as a whole. This pose a great challenge for us reach out to our learners again. This is our starting point to use the three great weapons in education – mind, heart and hand.

Let the battle to help our students reach for their dream begin.

BRAIN storming. We fight, not through our bodies, but, through our minds. Before we started the remedial reading classes, we conducted series of discussions and brainstorming to plan for the reading lessons and materials that we will use for every student depending on their level. It is a must that we know what to use to teach to every type of learner. In using the right ways, lessons and topics, we can assure that there is greater chance for our learners in achieving their academic goals.

We compose passion to show compassion. Aside from teaching the students about the lessons that they need to learn to improve their reading skills, we also speak from our heart and listen to their heart. To deal with these kinds of learners is very crucial because deep inside their mind and hearts they are struggling. They suffered from bullying because they cannot read. They are deeply hurt because they cannot focus on their lessons as a result of the poor situation of their family. They are agonizing because no one care about what they think and what they feel. In every remedial reading class we show to them that we are always hear to listen to them. Our poor reader are always motivated to attend their remedial reading classes because we do not just listen to what they read but also to their voices that are hiding. Our minds are always open to listen and our hearts are always open to show compassion.

Their lives are what they choose to make them. The real evidence of holistic development of a students is on how he use the things that he knows and feels in the real world. Education must get through the mind into the heart and hands. The practical applications of what the students have learned in our remedial reading classes are salient in seeing the effectiveness of the learning. We allow them to create an environment where they are not afraid to use the things that they have learned without our presence. With this, we are teaching our students that at the end of the day, their future is in their own hands.

This global pandemic that we are experiencing right now is one of the greatest threats to the education. Even we have this unfortunate situation, we never stopped in using the power of mind, heart and hand in reaching out for our poor readers. Our passion and eagerness to help them are always burning like a fire that will give light to the darkness that devoured their dreams. We will always hold the torch of wisdom, compassion and action up high so that its light will illuminate and bring brightness to the future of our students.

We are just poor teachers but through our mind, heart and hand we can make other people rich and reach for their dreams.

THE ART OF TEACHING

Chezza Maine P. Tugaoen

Can we step back for a moment and think about those times when the world is still in perfect shape? Do you see the days when our students greet us teachers every morning? Seeing the students having chitchats in the hallway? Entering the classroom, greet you with cheerful smiles?

What do you feel? Do you see yourself smiling upon recalling those moments?

Here and now, we wake up with dark circles under our eyes and glasses on. We step into the classroom, welcoming our learners thru our phones and laptops. As we look into it, those happy memories will remain memories. No more students' volunteers carrying our bags, and no more students running in the hallway. All that's left are the empty classrooms, the canteen that looks haunted, and the deserted books at the library.

The whole world was unprepared. Everything was so sudden. Teaching in the past is distinct from this present moment. Today's educational system focuses on distance learning modalities, such as online learning and modular.

Before we begin our class, we start with an end goal in mind.

As an educator, we must...

Prepare ourselves.

When we go to battle, we prepare ourselves. We are like soldiers, and our enemy is the epidemic. The firearm serves as our pen. Our eraser is the bomb, and the rucksack carries all our know-how. We, teachers, commit ourselves to the subjects that we are teaching and learn as much as possible to provide them the best education they deserve. We give our very best in teaching our learners and make them able to learn or master the skills, and turned them meaningful and applicable in real-life situations. A knowledgeable, confident, clever teacher but never arrogant is who prepares herself.

Prepare our learners.

"Educating the mind without educating the heart is no education at all" – Aristotle

We, teachers, reach out to our learners and make a difference in their lives. Teaching isn't just about teaching; we make sure that our learners truly learn and grow. We do not just cater their minds with the ABCs or prepare them on the assessments but preparing them at present and for their future life. I believed that success in teaching isn't all about head-to-head but heart-to-heart. We don't just teach, but we inspire and let them love learning because their dreams are our dreams as well.

Prepare our materials.

Materials aren't just all about the lesson plans or instructional materials. It involves our body and mind that emerged. We, teachers, provide our learners with minds-on, hearts-on, and hands-on experiences. It is what encourages our learners to experience and deeply engage in the learning process. When we prepare our materials, we learn and consider the interest of our learners.

Importantly, I should be the first to learn. Second, to inspire. Third, to act. The common ingredient is extending ourselves to help our students learn and grow.

In the end, the art of good teaching is within us.

BIOGRAPHY

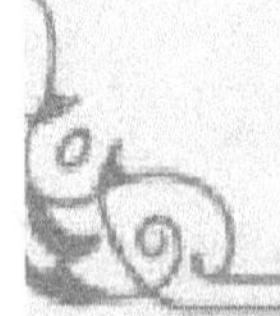

DR VERONICA F GUERRERO

DR. VERONICA F GUERRERO is a graduate of Bachelor of Secondary Education major in English and minor in Social Science; Master of Arts in Education- Educational Management; Doctor of Education- Educational Management. She teaches English, Spanish and Theater Arts; a renowned coach/trainer in public speaking and journalistic writing and a playwright/director in theater production; a member of the International Society of Teachers, Administrators and Researchers Inc. (ISTAR).

Dr. Guerrero was a scholarship grantee to the SEAMEO Short Term Course in Introduction to Computer/Internet Technology at the Nanyang University in Singapore; a foreign language

(Spanish) scholar at the Instituto Cervantes. She was awarded as Outstanding Master Teacher in the Division of Laoag City in 2016; an International Coach winner in essay writing; and a national Evaluator in English textbooks.

At present, she is the coordinator of the Debate Society, Special Program in Foreign Language-Spanish, and Special Program in the Arts- Theater Arts of the Ilocos Norte National High School. Also, she is a part time professor in the College of Education and in the Graduate School of Northwestern University in Laoag City.

SHELA MAE T. BORRO

Shela Mae T. Borro took Bachelor of Secondary Education Major in English at Cagayan State University – Sanchez Mira. She passed the Civil Service Examination – Professional in 2018 and also the Board Licensure Examination for Professional Teachers in 2019. She experienced working as a customer service representative and she is now a private school teacher at the Academy of St. Joseph, Claveria, Cagayan.

She is a devoted reader of Lang Leav's and Michael Faudet's literary works. She was inspired to be an author by these two. Through this book, she experienced being one. She views teaching as a lifelong commitment. She adopted her life's mantra in her first job which is Passion, Patience, and Perseverance. Later on, she learned the other two P's, Persistence and Purpose. She is applying these in her teaching career in nurturing not only the minds of the young learners but also their values in life.

LYNETH MELISSA M. CALAUTIT

Lyneth Melissa M. Calautit is a Junior High School English Teacher at Paoay National High School. A graduate in the degree of Bachelor in Secondary Education major in English. She is currently taking up Master of Arts in Education major in Language and Literature teaching at Northwestern University, Vedasto J. Samonte School of Graduate Studies. She is from Barangay 3 Alogoog, Badoc, Ilocos Norte.

ROXANNE A. CONSTANTINO

Roxanne A. Constantino currently teaches at Sta. Rosa National High School, her alma mater. She takes up her Master of Arts in Education Major in Language and Literature Teaching. She once dreamt of publishing a book with her name on it. Thank God for her Psycholinguistic class at Vedasto J. Samonte School of Graduate Studies, her dream has turned into reality. She is all the more inspired to write and to share her masterpieces.

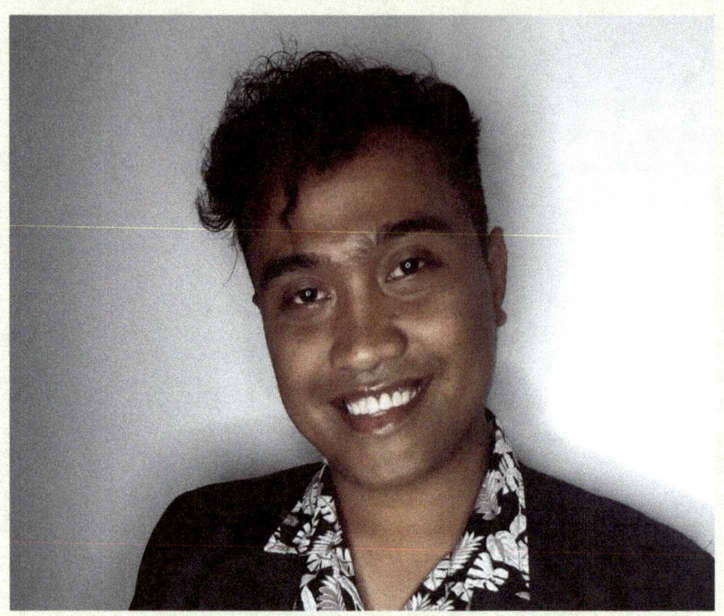

MARK ANGELO RIVERA DAMO

Mark Angelo Rivera Damo is a Senior High School English Language and Literature teacher of San Nicolas National High School, San Nicolas, Ilocos Norte. He graduated Cum Laude of the degree Bachelor in Secondary Education major in English at the Mariano Marcos State University-College of Teacher Education. He is a writer, book author, school paper adviser and campus journalism coach.

MELODY F. DAMULOG

Melody F. Damulog is a graduate of Bachelor of Science in Secondary Education, Major in English at Taguig City University - College of Education in the year 2015. She is currently the Junior High School English Teacher and Phil-Iri English Coordinator of Caribquib National High School, Banna, Ilocos Norte. She is one of the contributors of selected Title Proposals of Three Acts of Goodness and the SDOIN Tungtungan publication. She continues professional development at Northwestern University with the course, Masters of education – Major in language and Literature. Through the effort of Dr. Veronica F. Guerrero, her professor in Psycholinguistics and some veteran writers who happen to be her classmates, she has given an opportunity to continue her passion in writing.

ARJHONAMAE D. DOROTAN

Arjhonamae D. Dorotan is a graduate of Bachelor of Science in Industrial Education major in Technical Drafting at MMSU – College of Industrial Technology year 2014. As a teacher of Technical Drafting at Catagtaguen National High School for 5 years, she never thought that she could unluck her passion to be a writer. Thanks to her Psycholinguistics class under Dr. Veronica F. Guerrero as her professor at the Vedasto J. Samonte School of Graduate Studies at Northwestern University where she currently taking her Master of Education major in Educational Management for helping her turn her pencil and sketch pad into paper and ballpen where she can write with dedication and compassion.

JERICK T. GUIANG

Jerick T. Guiang is a coach in debate and oration, a research ethics committee member, and an events host. He is currently teaching and taking up his Master of Arts in Education Major in Language and Literature Teaching at the same time at Northwestern University. He has always been a speaker than a writer but because of his Psycholinguistics class in the Vedasto J. Samonte School of Graduate Studies, he then had the chance to be a writer accomplishing something that he never thought would happen.

JONATHAN AGASANG PAGUIRIGAN

Jonathan Agasang Paguirigan is a full-time instructor of the College of Arts and Sciences of Northwestern University. He is a graduate of Bachelor of Arts of English Studies and finished his 18-unit Professional Education course at Northwestern University, Laoag City. He successfully passed his Licensure Examination for Teacher in 2019. He is currently taking Master of Arts in Education, major in language and Literature, also in Northwestern University. He is also the concurrent Acting Cultural Affairs Coordinator of the said university from 2019 to the present. He is a native of Barangay 1, San Francisco San Nicolas, Ilocos Norte.

CINDIE R. LACRO

Cindie R. Lacro is a licensed teacher with Bachelor of Elementary Education from Mariano Marcos State University. She just started teaching at Paoay Faith Academy Inc. She is taking up Master of Arts in Education Major in Language and Literature Teaching at Northwestern University. At the age of twenty-two, she never imagined to write manuscript. She was grateful because she was able to experience new thing, thanks to her Psycholinguistics class at Vedasto J. Samonte School of Graduate Studies.

REIZEL ANN L. LUCERO

Reizel Ann L. Lucero is a Junior High School teacher of Paoay Lake National High School, Paoay, Ilocos Norte. She is currently teaching English Subjects and Chinese- Mandarin. A graduate of bachelor in Secondary Education major in English at the University of Northern Philippines, Vigan City and earned her units in Master of Arts in Teaching, Major in English at the same University. And now, she is currently taking up Master of Arts in Education Major in Language and Literature Teaching at Northwestern University, Laoag City.

RONALD M. MARCOS

Ronald Marcos holds a Teacher III position at Bangui National High School in Bangui, Ilocos Norte, Philippines. He assumes key roles in the academic and civic spheres as adviser of "Ang Banaag", the official publication (Filipino) of Bangui NHS, coordinator of the Parents-Teachers Association, founder of the SHARE to CARE program, and an active member of the Bangui United. As a school paper adviser and coach, he has helped produce winners in editorial and feature writing, and radio broadcasting. He was a former President of both KATAFIL (Kapisanan ng mga Tagapagtaguyod sa Filipino), Schools Division of Ilocos Norte and Bangui NHS Employees Association. He is a candidate of the Master of Arts in Education major in Educational Management program of Northwestern University, Laoag City.

KRISTAL ZANIAH V. RANADA

Kristal Zaniah V. Ranada believed that "Each student is capable of greatness". She graduated from Cagayan State University with a degree of Bachelor of Secondary Education. She is taking up Master of Arts in Education Major in Language and Literature Teaching at Northwestern University. Being a writer was her desire when she was in college, but now she accomplished and was able to show her manuscript unexpectedly, thanks to her Psycholinguistics class in the Vedasto J. Samonte School of Graduate Studies for making this possible.

JULIE ANN REYES SALAZAR

Julie Ann Reyes Salazar graduated at Mariano Marcos State University-College of Teacher Education where she attained bachelor's degree in Secondary Education major in English. In the four years in the field of education she has already taught English and Literature to the Grades 7 and 8 students of Piddig National High School where she is currently working as a faculty member, class adviser and newspaper adviser. She is presently taking up her master's degree in at Northwestern University Graduate School.

MISHELL T. SEVILLA

Mishell T. Sevilla is a Senior High School teacher of Piddig National High School. She teaches Oral Communication in Context and Reading and Writing Skills that provides her many opportunities to practice her enthusiasm in the English language as a writer and a radio broadcaster in the Division of Ilocos Norte. She finds teaching as a good chance to see connections with others for a transformative learning.

She obtained a bachelor's degree in Secondary Education major in English and Religious Education from the Divine Word College of Vigan. Her education trained her to be great educator who would be able to provide learners' need in varying situations.

SIMPLICIANO, JOHN JUFEL VALDEZ

Simpliciano, John Jufel Valdez is a Licensed Professional Teacher of San Nicolas National High School (SNNHS). Aside from being a classroom teacher, he is currently the coordinator of the SNNHS Remedial Reading Program which won First Runner Up in the 2019 Region I - Best Implementer of Bawat Bata Bumabasa last March 2019. He finished his Bachelor of Secondary Education degree major in English at Mariano Marcos State University – College of Teacher Education. He is currently taking up Master of Arts in Education major in Language and Literature Teaching at Vedasto J. Samonte School of Graduate Studies (VJSSGS) of Northwestern University (NWU) where he became the President of NWU-VJSSGS Student Council last School Year 2017-2018.

CHEZZA MAINE P. TUGAOEN

Chezza Maine P. Tugaoen, age 22. She's into dancing, sketching, and writing stories. She started as a tutor of three English-speaking students in her hometown, Pinili, Ilocos Norte. She holds a degree of Bachelor of Elementary Education, Major in General Education, which she earned at Mariano Marcos State University, College of Teacher Education, Laoag City. At present, she is taking up a Master of Arts in Education - Language and Literature Teaching at Vedasto J. Samonte School of Graduate Studies.